NAPOLEON HILL'S

Daily
Inspiration
for All
SEASONS

Compiled and edited by
Judith Williamson

A publication of
THE NAPOLEON HILL FOUNDATION

Published by:

The Napoleon Hill Foundation
P. O. Box 1277
Wise, Virginia USA 24293

Website: www.naphill.org
Email: napoleonhill@uvawise.edu

Quotations written by Napoleon Hill and others.

Compiled and edited by Judith A. Williamson, Director
Napoleon Hill World Learning Center
Purdue University Calumet
2300 173rd Street
Hammond, Indiana 46323
Email: nhf@calumet.purdue.edu

ISBN: 978-0-9819511-8-8

Introduction

Napoleon Hill's Daily Inspiration for all Seasons is comprised of a selected daily quotation by the great author of *Think and Grow Rich.* Readers can use these quotations drawn from both the writings of Dr. Hill and matched with those of other writers to inspire them through each season of success. These inspirational quotes may be likened to a treasure map that keeps the reader headed in the right direction as they journey onward. Sometimes that little extra push gives a person the necessary drive to go the distance. These quotations are like fuel for the trip. Read the daily quotations, reflect on the message, and take appropriate action. Remember, you must continue through each season until you arrive at your destination. Enjoy the success that you are striving for in all seasons of your life. Remember too, that life's riches are not only financial, but mental, spiritual, emotional, social, and physical. Keep that in mind as you travel through each season of growth. Consider the multiple riches that every season has to offer. In discussing life's riches, Dr. Hill states: *We can become complete masters of ourselves, if we so desire. The main thought to bear in mind is first to gain the knowledge, and secondly to apply it.*

Be your very best always in all ways!
Judith Williamson
Director: Napoleon Hill World Learning Center

January

You can always become
the person you would have
liked to be.

—NAPOLEON HILL

January 1

Every person who wins in any undertaking must be willing to burn his ships and cut all sources of retreat.

—NAPOLEON HILL

Act in spite of fear.

–CHARLIE TREMENDOUS JONES

January 2

From winding pathways or straight,
every thought you send out, every
deed you perform, will gather a
flock of other thoughts or deeds
according to its own nature, and
come back home to you in due time.
—NAPOLEON HILL

The one and only formative power
given to man is thought. By his
thinking he not only makes character,
but body and affairs, for as he
thinketh within himself, so is he.
—CHARLES FILLMORE

~ Day 2 ~

January 3

Wise men share most of their riches generously. They share their confidences sparingly, and take great care not to misplace them. And when they talk of their aims and plans they generally do it by action rather than by words.

—NAPOLEON HILL

The sole meaning of life is to serve humanity.

—LEO TOLSTOY

January 4

*The space you occupy and the
authority you exercise may be
measured with mathematical
exactness by the service you render.*
—NAPOLEON HILL

*The making of money, the
accumulation of material power,
is not all there is to living. Life
is something more than these,
and the man who misses this
truth misses the greatest joy and
satisfaction that can come into his
life—service for others.*
—EDWARD W. BOK

~ Day 4 ~

January 5

The persistent man with a poor plan stands a better chance of winning than the man with a perfect plan who hesitates and waivers in carrying it out.

—NAPOLEON HILL

By perseverance the snail reached the Ark.

—CHARLES SPURGEON

January 6

*A man without enthusiasm or a
Definite Major Purpose resembles
a locomotive without either steam
or a track on which to run, or a
destination toward which to travel.*
—NAPOLEON HILL

*The man without a purpose is
like a ship without a rudder—a
waif, a nothing, a no man. Have
a purpose in life, and, having it,
throw such strength of mind and
muscle into your work as God has
given you.*
—THOMAS CARLYLE

January 7

It will make a big difference to you whether you are a person with a message or a person with a grievance.

—NAPOLEON HILL

Nothing can stop the man with the right mental attitude from achieving his goal; nothing on earth can help the man with the wrong mental attitude.

–W. W. ZIEGE

~ Day 7 ~

January 8

*Initiative means the doing of things
without being told to do them.*
—NAPOLEON HILL

*A man who gives his children habits
of industry provides for them better
than by giving them a fortune.*
–RICHARD WHATELY

January 9

There are no lazy men. What
may appear to be a lazy man is
only an unfortunate person who
has not found the work for
which he is best suited.

—NAPOLEON HILL

No wind favors him who
has no destined port.

—MICHEL DE MONTAIGNE

January 10

I give thanks daily, not for more riches, but for wisdom with which to recognize, embrace and properly use the great abundance of riches I now have at my command.
—NAPOLEON HILL

One can never pay in gratitude; one can only pay in kind somewhere else in life.
—ANNE MORROW LINDBERGH

~ Day 10 ~

January 11

Success is good at any age, but the sooner you find it, the longer you will enjoy it.

—NAPOLEON HILL

In achieving success, backbone is more important than wishbone.

—FRANK TYGER

January 12

We cannot sow thistles and reap clover. Nature simply does not run things that way. She goes by cause and effect.
—NAPOLEON HILL

In nature there are neither rewards nor punishments, there are consequences.
—ROBERT G. INGERSOLL

January 13

Defeat may break up some negative habit one has formed, thus releasing one's energies for the formation of other and more desirable habits.

—NAPOLEON HILL

Our greatest glory is not in never falling, but in rising every time we fall.

—CONFUCIUS

January 14

*A man always does his best
work when he feels that he is
acting upon his own initiative
and knows he must assume full
responsibility for his action.*

—NAPOLEON HILL

*National progress is the sum
of individual industry, energy,
and uprightness, as national decay
is of individual idleness,
selfishness, and vice.*

—SAMUEL SMILES

~ Day 14 ~

January 15

*Power may be defined as
"organized and intelligently
directed knowledge."*
—Napoleon Hill

*Find your advantage or
someone will take it away.*
—Joe Dudley

January 16

*I know I am here. I know I
had nothing to do with my
coming, and I shall have but little,
if anything, to do with my going,
therefore I will not worry because
worries are of no avail.*
—NAPOLEON HILL

*Worry, whatever its source,
weakens, takes away courage,
and shortens life.*
–JOHN LANCASTER SPALDING

~ Day 16 ~

January 17

*Hurry! The sand in your hourglass
is running lower every second, and
the glass can't be refilled.*
—NAPOLEON HILL

*Waste neither time nor money,
but make the best use of both.*
—BENJAMIN FRANKLIN

January 18

*We have no trouble in giving
feeling to speech when we believe
what we are saying!*
—Napoleon Hill

*Our lives begin to end the
day we become silent about
things that matter.*
–Martin Luther King, Jr.

January 19

*Remember that your real wealth
can be measured, not by what you
have, but, by what you are.*
—NAPOLEON HILL

*A man's true wealth is the
good he does in this world.*
—MUHAMMAD

January 20

Through some strange and powerful principle of "mental chemistry" which she has never divulged, Nature wraps up in the impulse of strong desire "that something" which recognizes no such word as impossible, and accepts no such reality as failure.

—NAPOLEON HILL

I love to think of nature as an unlimited broadcasting station, through which God speaks to us every hour, if we will only tune in.

—GEORGE WASHINGTON CARVER

~ Day 20 ~

January 21

*It has been said, and perhaps
correctly, that "courtesy" represents
the most valuable characteristic
known to the human race.*
—NAPOLEON HILL

*Depend not on fortune,
but on conduct.*
—PUBLILIUS SYRUS

January 22

We climb to heaven mostly on
the ruins of our cherished plans,
finding our failures were but
friendly guide-posts that led us
onward and upward to success.

—NAPOLEON HILL

Great men are very apt to have
great faults; and the faults appear
the greater by their contrast with
their excellencies.

–GERALD J. SIMMONS

~ Day 22 ~

January 23

Start right where you stand, now!
—NAPOLEON HILL

*One must learn by doing the thing,
for though you think you know it,
you have no certainty until you try.*
—ARISTOTLE

January 24

*Thought "magnetizes" one's
entire physical body, and attracts
to one the outward, physical things
which harmonize.*

—NAPOLEON HILL

*There are two distinct classes
of what are called thoughts: those
that we produce in ourselves by
reflection and the act of thinking
and those that bolt into the mind of
their own accord.*

—THOMAS PAINE

~ Day 24 ~

January 25

*A master salesman is an artist
who can paint word-pictures in
the hearts of men as skillfully as
Rembrandt could blend colors
on a canvas.*

—NAPOLEON HILL

*We are all salesmen every day of
our lives. We are selling our ideas,
our plans, our enthusiasms to those
with whom we come in contact.*

—CHARLES M. SCHWAB

~ Day 25 ~

January 26

*Do not "tell" the world what
you can do—"Show" it!*
—NAPOLEON HILL

*It is well to think well;
it is divine to act well.*
—HORACE MANN

January 27

*The Master Key is intangible,
but it is powerful! It is the privilege
of creating in your own mind, a
burning desire for a definite
form of riches.*

—NAPOLEON HILL

*Ah, but a man's reach should exceed
his grasp. Or what's a heaven for?*

—ROBERT BROWNING

January 28

*You cannot entirely control
your subconscious mind, but
you can voluntarily hand over
to it any plan, desire, or purpose
which you wish transformed
into concrete form.*
—NAPOLEON HILL

*Don't quit five minutes
before the miracle happens.*
—RUDY RUETTIGER

January 29

It is better to be too big for your job than to have a job that is too big for you.

—Napoleon Hill

The highest reward for a person's toil is not what he gets for it, but what he becomes by it.

–John Ruskin

~ Day 29 ~

January 30

A mind dominated by positive emotions, becomes a favorable abode for the state of mind known as faith.

—NAPOLEON HILL

No ray of sunlight is ever lost, but the green which it awakes into existence needs time to sprout, and it is not always granted to the sower to see the harvest. All work that is worth anything is done in faith.

—ALBERT SCHWEITZER

~ Day 30 ~

January 31

*One sound idea is all that
one needs to achieve success.*
—NAPOLEON HILL

*You must believe it
before you can see it.*
–DON GREEN

February

Successful people move on their own initiative and they know where they are going before they start.

—NAPOLEON HILL

February 1

"What helped you over the great obstacles of life?" was asked of a highly successful man. "The other obstacles," he replied.
—NAPOLEON HILL

Refuse to surrender.
—FRANK MAGUIRE

February 2

It may not be literally true that "thoughts are things" but it is true that thoughts create all things, and the things they create are striking duplicates of the thought-patterns from which they are fashioned.

—NAPOLEON HILL

The happiness of your life depends upon the quality of your thoughts.

— MARCUS AURELIUS

February 3

Faith is guidance from within! The guiding force is Infinite Intelligence directed to definite ends. It will not bring that which one desires, but it will guide one to the attainment of the object of desire.

—Napoleon Hill

Faith is the great motive power, and no man realizes his full possibilities unless he has the deep conviction that life is eternally important and that his work well done is a part of an unending plan.

—Calvin Coolidge

February 4

The major weakness of most men is that they recognize the obstacles they must surmount without recognizing the spiritual power at their command by which those obstacles may be removed at will.

—NAPOLEON HILL

The block of granite which was an obstacle in the path of the weak, becomes a steppingstone in the path of the strong.

–THOMAS CARLYLE

~ Day 35 ~

February 5

The seventeen principles will serve as a dependable roadmap leading directly to the source of all riches, whether they are intangible or material riches.

—NAPOLEON HILL

Nothing can stand in the way of passion.

—JULIE KRONE

February 6

Remember that your mind guides you toward the thing you think about most. Spend no time, therefore, in thinking of the things you DO NOT WANT, for this is precisely the same as hoping and wishing for the things you do not want.

—NAPOLEON HILL

He that will not command his thoughts will soon lose the command of his actions.

—WOODROW WILSON

~ Day 37 ~

February 7

*When you run out of something
to do, try your hand at writing
down a list of all the reasons why
the world needs you. The
experiment may surprise you.*

—Napoleon Hill

*It is difficult to make a man
miserable while he feels he is
worthy of himself and claims
kindred to the great God who
made him.*

—Abraham Lincoln

~ Day 38 ~

February 8

Life, you can't subdue me,
because I refuse to take your
discipline seriously.
—NAPOLEON HILL

A true man never frets about his
place in the world, but just slides
into it by the gravitation of his
nature, and swings there as easily
as a star.
—EDWIN H. CHAPIN

February 9

Everywhere, regardless of the form in which it is found, power is developed through concentrated energy. Whatever you are doing as your daily occupation, do it with all of your attention, all your heart and soul focused on the one definite thing.

—NAPOLEON HILL

Responsibilities gravitate to the person who can shoulder them; power flows to the man who knows how.

—ELBERT HUBBARD

February 10

*Is it not strange that nowhere
in history do we find a record
of one great man who attained
his greatness through deceit,
trickery, and by double-crossing
his business associates?*

—NAPOLEON HILL

*I hope you have not been leading a
double life, pretending to be wicked,
and being really good all the time.
That would be hypocrisy.*

—OSCAR WILDE

February 11

*Unfed worry soon
dies of starvation.*

—Napoleon Hill

*As a cure for worrying,
work is better than whiskey.*

—Thomas Edison

February 12

*Life has no bargain counters.
Everything has a price which must
be paid in one form or another. No
man is smart enough to cheat Life.
It has been tried by the smartest of
men without success.*

—NAPOLEON HILL

*If you intend to go to work, there
is no better place than right where
you are; if you do not intend to go
to work, you cannot get along
anywhere. Squirming and
crawling about from place to
place can do no good.*

—ABRAHAM LINCOLN

~ Day 43 ~

February 13

It is well-known fact that one man, whose mental attitude is negative, if he is in a position of authority, will project his influence down into the rank and file of an entire organization of men, so changing their mental attitude as to make them dissatisfied and, therefore, inefficient in their work.

—Napoleon Hill

The greatest revelation of our generation is the discovery that human beings, by changing the inner attitudes of their minds, can change the outer aspects of their lives.

—William James

February 14

*Ability to influence people
without irritating them is the most
profitable art known to man.*
—Napoleon Hill

*Our attitude is determined by 10%
of what life hands you, and 90% of
how you choose to respond.*
–John Hope Bryant

~ Day 45 ~

February 15

*The man who sows a single
beautiful thought in the mind
of another renders the world,
through that act, a greater service
than that rendered by all the
fault-finders combined.*

—NAPOLEON HILL

*Believe in yourself, and the
world will believe in you!*

–JIM OLESON

February 16

*No man can become a great leader
of men unless he has the milk of
human kindness in his own heart,
and leads by suggestion and
kindness, rather than by force.*
—NAPOLEON HILL

*Kindness in words creates
confidence, kindness in thinking
creates profoundness, kindness in
giving creates love.*
—LAO-TZU

February 17

You can do it if you believe you can.
—Napoleon Hill

*When you affirm big, believe big,
and pray big, big things happen.*
—Norman Vincent Peale

~ *Day* 48 ~

February 18

There comes to your aid,
and to do your bidding, with the
development of the sixth sense,
a "guardian angel" who will open
to you at all times the door to the
temple of wisdom.

—NAPOLEON HILL

Great men are they who see that
spiritual is stronger than any
material force; that thoughts rule
the world.

—RALPH WALDO EMERSON

~ Day 49 ~

February 19

*Your first step on the road to
Success is to know where you are
going, how you intend to travel,
and when you intend to get there,
which is only another way of
saying that you must determine
upon a definite chief aim.*

—NAPOLEON HILL

*Success is not a matter of desire,
but the product of hard work.*

—JACK BARRINGER

~ *Day 50* ~

February 20

*The best compensation for doing
things is the ability to do more.*
—NAPOLEON HILL

*One only gets to the top rung on
the ladder by steadily climbing up
one at a time, and suddenly all
sorts of powers, all sort of abilities
which you thought never belonged
to you—suddenly become within
your own possibility and you think,
"Well, I'll have a go, too."*
—MARGARET THATCHER

~ Day 51 ~

February 21

*If you do not believe in
co-operation, look what happens
to a wagon that loses a wheel.*
—NAPOLEON HILL

*Two men working as a team
will produce more than three men
working as individuals.*
—CHARLES P. MCCORMICK

February 22

Every spoken word leaves its
footprints upon the speaker's mind
and becomes a part of his character.

—NAPOLEON HILL

Ninety-nine percent of the
failures come from people who have
the habit of making excuses.

—GEORGE WASHINGTON

February 23

It is one of the great tragedies of civilization that ninety-eight out of every one hundred persons go all the way through life without coming within sight of anything that even approximates definiteness of a major purpose.

—NAPOLEON HILL

A purpose is the eternal condition of success.

—THEODORE T. MUNGER

February 24

Adversity is to the human being what the kiln is to the brick—it tempers the man so he can carry responsibilities and overcome obstacles without crumbling before them.

—Napoleon Hill

Adversity has the effect of eliciting talents which in prosperous circumstances would have lain dormant.

—Horace

~ Day 55 ~

February 25

It is well worth remembering that the customer is the most important factor in any business. If you don't think so, try to get along without him for a while.

—Napoleon Hill

If it is not in the interest of the public it is not in the interest of business.

–Joseph H. Defrees

February 26

*Building a better mouse trap
than one's neighbor will avail one
nothing unless sound, intense, and
continuous sales promotion is
placed back of the trap.*
—NAPOLEON HILL

*All men's gains are
the fruit of venturing.*
—HERODOTUS

February 27

There is a mistaken idea floating
around that a man should be paid
for that which he knows. In reality
a man is paid for that which he does
with what he knows, or that which
he can get others to do with it.

—Napoleon Hill

Knowledge is a treasure
but practice is the key to it.

—Thomas Fuller

~ Day 58 ~

February 28

*At the onset let us define success
as: "The power with which to
acquire whatever one wants
without violating the rights
of others."*
—Napoleon Hill

*Success is simple. Do what's right,
the right way, at the right time.*
–Arnold Glasow

~ Day 59 ~

March

When you share with others
a part of what you have, that
which remains will multiply
and grow.

—NAPOLEON HILL

March 1

A person with positive mental attitude aims for high goals and constantly strives to achieve them.

—Napoleon Hill

An aim in life is the only fortune worth the finding.

—Robert Louis Stevenson

~ Day 60 ~

March 2

Fortunes gravitate to men whose minds have been prepared to attract them, just as surely as water gravitates to the ocean.

—NAPOLEON HILL

There is the tide in the affairs of men, which, taken at the flood, leads on to fortune; omitted, all the voyage of their life is bound in shallows and in miseries.

—WILLIAM SHAKESPEARE

March 3

A group of brains coordinated in a spirit of harmony will provide more thought energy than a single brain, just as a group of electric batteries will provide more energy than a single battery.

—NAPOLEON HILL

Great discoveries and improvements invariably involve the co-operation of many minds. I may be given credit for having blazed the trail but when I look at the subsequent developments I feel the credit is due to others rather than to myself.

—ALEXANDER GRAHAM BELL

March 4

*Convert what you see
into reality by action.*
—NAPOLEON HILL

*Great thoughts reduced to
practice become great acts.*
–WILLIAM HAZLITT

March 5

Physical pain is the universal language in which Mother Nature speaks to every creature on earth, and it is understood and respected by all.

—NAPOLEON HILL

The secret of health for both mind and body is not to mourn the past, not to worry about the future, not to anticipate troubles, but to live the present moment wisely and earnestly.

–BUDDHA

~ Day 64 ~

March 6

Success requires no explanations.
Failure permits no alibis.
—NAPOLEON HILL

As the plant springs from, and
could not be without the seed, so
every act of a man springs from the
hidden seeds of thought and could
not have appeared without them.
–JAMES ALLEN

March 7

*Fears are nothing more
than states of mind.*
—Napoleon Hill

*Present fears are less
than horrible imaginings.*
—William Shakespeare

March 8

The real test of a man's belief in a positive mental attitude and of his faith is in the challenge of change which he must meet every day of his life.
—Napoleon Hill

Observe constantly that all things take place by change.
–Marcus Aurelius

March 9

When defeat overtakes you, don't
spend all your time counting your
losses. Save some of it to count
your gains and you may find they
are greater than your losses.

—NAPOLEON HILL

Every problem contains a gift.

–RICHARD BACH

March 10

Know what you want; then begin,
right where you stand, to visualize
yourself as being already in
possession of it.

—Napoleon Hill

Dream lofty dreams and as
you dream, so shall you become.

–James Allen

March 11

A sense of guilt is good. And every living person regardless of how good or bad he may be will sometimes experience a feeling of guilt.

—NAPOLEON HILL

A failure is a man who has blundered but is not able to cash in on the experience.

—ELBERT HUBBARD

~ Day 70 ~

March 12

Definiteness of Purpose:
This is the arrow
aimed toward the goal.
—NAPOLEON HILL

There are two things to aim at
in life; first, to get what you want;
and after that, to enjoy it. Only
the wisest of mankind achieve
the second.
—LOGAN PEARSALL SMITH

March 13

*Every defeat that you meet will
mark an important turning point
in your life, for defeat will bring
you face to face with the necessity
of renewing confidence in yourself,
or of admitting that confidence
is lacking.*

—NAPOLEON HILL

*Patience and perseverance
have a magical effect before which
difficulties disappear and
obstacles vanish.*

—JOHN QUINCY ADAMS

March 14

As we are one with the world about us, so are we one with ourselves: a mind-body.
—NAPOLEON HILL

Everyone who is seriously involved in the pursuit of science becomes convinced that a Spirit is manifest in the Laws of the Universe—a Spirit vastly superior to that of man, and one in the face of which we with our modest powers, must feel humble.
—ALBERT EINSTEIN

~ Day 73 ~

March 15

Send out positive thoughts from a positively oriented soul and the world will reflect back greater and greater positive influences to help you.

—Napoleon Hill

*My mind is a garden.
My thoughts are the seeds.
My harvest will be either
flowers or weeds.*

—Mel Weldon

March 16

*Keep your mind so busy doing
the things you want to do that no
time will be left for it to stray into
the things you do not want.*
—NAPOLEON HILL

*Dream big, and never stop
short of reaching the top.*
—TRUETT CATHY

March 17

Our attitudes shape our future.
—Napoleon Hill

*The last of the human
freedoms—to choose one's attitude
in any given set of circumstances,
to choose one's own way.*
—Viktor E. Frankl

March 18

The majority of people who fail to accumulate money sufficient to their needs are, generally, easily influenced by the opinions of others.

—NAPOLEON HILL

People simply need to replace their wishbone with a backbone.

–JOHN ST. AUGUSTINE

March 19

Positive Mental Attitude:
We cannot NOT do anything.
Being negative is doing something.
To govern your life, you must learn
to govern your attitudes.

—NAPOLEON HILL

The idea is to seek a vision that
gives you purpose in life and then to
implement that vision.

–LEWIS P. JOHNSON

March 20

*If your education consists solely
of what you have learned from
books, it will not be complete until
you have had the post-graduate
course in experience.*

—Napoleon Hill

*What we learn to do,
we learn by doing.*

—Aristotle

March 21

*Leadership can best be inspired
by planting in a man's mind a
definite motive that forces him to
acquire the qualities of leadership.
The profit motive is one of the
most popular.*

—NAPOLEON HILL

*Every wealth creator is crystal
clear about two things:
their vision and their mission.*

—TRUETT CATHY

March 22

*Self-discipline is the first rule
of all successful leadership.*
—Napoleon Hill

*Do not wait for leaders.
Do it alone, person to person.*
—Mother Teresa

March 23

The power of thought is the most mysterious and the greatest of all powers available. It can be the most beneficial, or the most dangerous, depending upon how it is used.

—NAPOLEON HILL

You are today where your thoughts have brought you; you will be tomorrow where your thoughts take you.

–JAMES ALLEN

~ Day 82 ~

March 24

Every time you perform a task,
try to excel your last performance,
and very soon you will excel
those around you.
—NAPOLEON HILL

Nothing will come of nothing.
Dare mighty things.
—WILLIAM SHAKESPEARE

March 25

Let it be remembered that the space one occupies in the hearts of others is determined precisely by the service he renders through some form of sharing.

—NAPOLEON HILL

At the day of judgment we shall not be asked what we have read but what we have done.

–THOMAS A. KEMPIS

~ Day 84 ~

March 26

*Successful men, in all callings,
never stop acquiring specialized
knowledge related to their major
purpose, business, or profession.*
—NAPOLEON HILL

*I know of no more encouraging
fact than the unquestionable ability
of man to elevate his life by a
conscious endeavor.*
–HENRY DAVID THOREAU

March 27

When things become so bad they
cannot become worse, they usually
begin to be better.

—NAPOLEON HILL

The gem cannot be polished
without friction, nor man
perfected without trials.

—CONFUCIUS

March 28

Day by day in every way through the grace of God I am getting better and better through PMA.

—NAPOLEON HILL

A nail is driven out by another nail, habit is overcome by habit.

—ERASMUS

March 29

The important thing after
setting a goal is taking action.

—NAPOLEON HILL

Perseverance is a great element
of success. If you only knock long
enough and loud enough at the gate,
you are sure to wake up somebody.

—HENRY WADSWORTH LONGFELLOW

March 30

Happiness is an elusive, transitory thing. And if you set out to search for it, you will find it evasive. But if you try to bring happiness to someone else, then it comes to you.

—NAPOLEON HILL

The grand essentials to happiness in this life are something to do, something to love, and something to hope for.

–JOSEPH ADDISON

March 31

In your search for the secret
of the method, do not look for a
miracle, because you will not find
it. You will find only the eternal
laws of nature.

—NAPOLEON HILL

If I believe I cannot do something,
it makes me incapable of doing it.
But when I believe I can, then I
acquire the ability to do it, even if
I did not have the ability in the
beginning.

—MAHATMA GHANDI

April

Faith is the art of believing by doing. It comes as a result of persistent action and cannot exist at the same time as fear.

—Napoleon Hill

April 1

It's not the epitaph on your
tombstone but the record of
your deeds that may perpetuate
your name after death.

—NAPOLEON HILL

We judge ourselves by what we feel
capable of doing, while others judge
us by what we have already done.

—HENRY WADSWORTH LONGFELLOW

April 2

*Self-mastery is the hardest
job you will ever tackle. If you
do not conquer self, you will
be conquered by self.*
—NAPOLEON HILL

*The person who has never
made a mistake will never make
anything else.*
–GEORGE BERNARD SHAW

April 3

*If you don't believe in yourself,
how can you ask others to do so?*
—Napoleon Hill

*To be what we are, and to become
what we are capable of becoming, is
the only end of life.*
—Robert Louis Stevenson

April 4

Your brain is both a broadcasting
station and a receiving station for
vibrations of thought, both positive
and negative.

—NAPOLEON HILL

When one commits an act,
one becomes the heir to that act.

–SHAKYAMUNI

April 5

*Learn to use the winds of
adversity to sail your ship of life!*
—NAPOLEON HILL

*One does not discard gold
because the bag holding it is dirty . . .
One does not refuse to gather
lotuses because the water in which
they grow is unclean.*
—NICHIREN

April 6

*One of the most common causes
of failure is the habit of quitting
when one is overtaken by
temporary defeat.*
—Napoleon Hill

*Have patience with all things,
but chiefly with yourself. Have
courage in considering your own
imperfections and instantly set
about improving yourself.
Every day begins anew.*
–St. Francis de Sales

April 7

Search until you find the point of approach to that secret power from within, and when you find it you will have discovered your true self—that "other self" which makes use of every experience of life.

—NAPOLEON HILL

Know thyself.

—SOCRATES

April 8

The only permanent thing in the entire universe is change. Nothing is the same for two consecutive days.
—NAPOLEON HILL

Life is a succession of lessons which must be lived to be understood.
—RALPH WALDO EMERSON

April 9

*Great fortunes or modest fortunes
are a blessing only when they are
used in good part to benefit others.*
—NAPOLEON HILL

*The purpose of life is not to win.
The purpose of life is to grow and to
share. When you come to look back
on all that you have done in life,
you will get more satisfaction from
the pleasure you have brought into
other people's lives than you will
from the time that you outdid and
defeated them.*
—RABBI HAROLD KUSHNER

~ Day 99 ~

April 10

It's a sure thing that you will not finish if you don't start. The most difficult part of any job is getting started.

—NAPOLEON HILL

If you follow your bliss, you put yourself on a kind of track that has been there all the while, waiting for you, and the life that you ought to be living.

–JOSEPH CAMPBELL

April 11

*Deal more with practice
and less with theory.*

—Napoleon Hill

*If you want a thing done,
do it yourself.*

—Jean Jacques Rousseau

April 12

The greatest application of applied faith is learning the art of keeping your mind focused on what you want.

—NAPOLEON HILL

People do not lack strength; they lack will.

—VICTOR HUGO

April 13

Anything in life worth
having is worth working for.
—Napoleon Hill

Far and away the best prize
that life offers is the chance to work
hard at work worth doing.
—Theodore Roosevelt

April 14

Your real wealth can be measured
not by what you have, but by what
you are.

—NAPOLEON HILL

Wealth is a dangerous inheritance,
unless the inheritor is trained to
active benevolence.

–CHARLES SIMMONS

April 15

You are what you are and where you are because of your established habits of thoughts and deeds.

—NAPOLEON HILL

Thought means life, since those who do not think do not live in any high or real sense. Thinking makes the man.

—AMOS BRONSON ALCOTT

April 16

Permanent success will remain beyond reach until you begin to look in the mirror for the real cause of your mistakes.

—NAPOLEON HILL

He who never made a mistake never made a discovery.

—SAMUEL SMILES

April 17

The turning point in the lives of those who succeed usually comes at the moment of some crisis, through which they are introduced to their "other selves."

—NAPOLEON HILL

Until you try, you don't know what you can't do.

—HENRY JAMES

April 18

When riches begin to come
they come so quickly, in such great
abundance, that one wonders where
they have been hiding during all
those lean years.

—NAPOLEON HILL

Come with us to the field, or go
with our brothers to the sea and
cast your net. For the land and the
sea shall be bountiful to you even
as to us.

—KAHLIL GIBRAN

April 19

A weak plan often succeeds through strong enthusiasm!
—NAPOLEON HILL

Enthusiasm is at the bottom of all progress. With it there is accomplishment. Without it there are only alibis.
—HENRY FORD

April 20

*PMA is the right mental
attitude for each specific occasion.*
—NAPOLEON HILL

*Your living is determined not so
much by what life brings to you as
by the attitude you bring to life;
not so much by what happens
to you as by the way your mind
looks at what happens.*
—JOHN HOMER MILLER

April 21

Power is organized knowledge expressed through intelligent efforts.

—Napoleon Hill

A great man is one who can have power and not abuse it.

—Henry L. Doherty

April 22

You are a mind with a body.
—Napoleon Hill

The sound body is the
product of the sound mind.
—George Bernard Shaw

April 23

There is a difference between wishing for a thing and being ready to receive it. No one is ready for a thing, until they believe they can acquire it.

—NAPOLEON HILL

For success, attitude is equally as important as ability.

—HARRY F. BANKS

~ Day 113 ~

April 24

The law of compensation isn't always swift, but it is as certain as the setting of the sun.

—NAPOLEON HILL

People think of the Golden Rule as something mild and innocuous, like a baby lamb. But when they suffer an infringement of it, they think they've been mauled by a panther.

—FRANCIS WREN

April 25

*Good deeds are of more
benefit than good intentions.*
—Napoleon Hill

*The smallest actual good is better
than the most magnificent promise
of impossibilities.*
–Thomas B. Macaulay

April 26

The subconscious mind will translate into reality a thought driven by fear just as readily as it will translate into reality a thought driven by courage, or faith.

—NAPOLEON HILL

If a man harbors any sort of fear, it percolates through all his thinking, damages his personality, makes him landlord to a ghost.

–LLOYD C. DOUGLAS

April 27

*The more you give, the
more comes back to you.*

—Napoleon Hill

*We make a living by what we get,
we make a life by what we give.*

—Winston Churchill

April 28

An educated person is not
necessarily the one who has
the knowledge, but the one who
knows where to get it when needed.
—Napoleon Hill

They know enough
who know how to learn.
—Henry Adams

The person who remains at the job until the work is finished, who performs a little more than is expected, is the one who will succeed.

—NAPOLEON HILL

In the ordinary business of life, industry can do anything which genius can do, and very many things which it cannot.

—HENRY WARD BEECHER

April 30

Cherish your visions and your dreams as they are the children of your soul; the blue-prints of your ultimate achievements.
—NAPOLEON HILL

Hold fast to dreams, for if dreams die, life is a broken-winged bird that cannot fly.
—LANGSTON HUGHES

May

You are not greater than
the thoughts that dominate
your mind.

—Napoleon Hill

May 1

Avoid all negative mental influences and especially avoid that shadow of mournful regret which can keep all the sunshine out of your life—and keep out other gold as well.

—NAPOLEON HILL

Pray look better, sir. Those things yonder are no giants, but windmills.

—SANCHO PANZA

May 2

You must either take charge of your mind and, by controlled attention, feed it the type of food you wish to produce, or you must pay the penalty of having your mind taken over by the negative influences of your environment.

—NAPOLEON HILL

Determine that the thing can and shall be done, and then we shall find the way.

—ABRAHAM LINCOLN

May 3

*Most people go through life by the line
of least resistance in every circumstance
where they can make a choice. They do
not recognize that following the line of
least resistance makes all rivers, and
some men, crooked!*

—NAPOLEON HILL

*If ever this free people, if
this Government itself is utterly
demoralized, it will come from this
incessant human wriggle and struggle
for office, which is but a way to live
without work.*

—ABRAHAM LINCOLN

May 4

Only those who have the habit of going the second mile ever find the end of the rainbow!

—NAPOLEON HILL

When you discover your mission, you will feel its demand. It will fill you with enthusiasm and a burning desire to get to work on it.

–W. CLEMENT STONE

May 5

Sound health begins with a "health consciousness," the product of a mind which thinks in terms of health and not in terms of illness. Plus temperance and moderation in eating, and in the balancing of physical activities.

—NAPOLEON HILL

A healthy body is a guest-chamber for the soul; a sick body is a prison.

–SIR FRANCIS BACON

May 6

Enthusiasm may be expressed in two ways: passively, through the stimulation of emotional feeling which inspires you to meditate and think in silence; and actively, by the expression of such feeling through words and deeds.

—NAPOLEON HILL

I found that the men and women who got to the top were those who did the jobs they had in hand, with everything they had of energy and enthusiasm and hard work.

–HARRY S. TRUMAN

May 7

Do the thing you like best and your life will be thereby enriched, your soul will be embellished, and you will be an inspiration for hope and faith and encouragement to all with whom you come into contact.

—Napoleon Hill

This above all: to thine own self be true. And it must follow as the night the day, thou canst not then be false to any man.

—William Shakespeare

May 8

To love praise, but not worship it,
and fear condemnation, but not go
down under it, is evidence of a
well balanced personality.

—NAPOLEON HILL

A pessimist is one who makes
difficulties of his opportunities and
an optimist is one who makes
opportunities of his difficulties.

–HARRY S. TRUMAN

May 9

*The motto of the person
who has his ego under control is
"Deeds, not words."*

—Napoleon Hill

*Such as thy words are, such will
thine affections be esteemed; and
such as thine affections, will be thy
deeds; and such as thy deeds
will be thy life.*

—Socrates

May 10

In essence, sex transmutation
is the ability to switch a desire for
physical contact to a similar desire
for expression—in art, literature,
science, selling or anything else.
—NAPOLEON HILL

Art, like morality, consists
of drawing the line somewhere.
–G. K. CHESTERTON

May 11

*The words are the media
through which a man most often
expresses his thoughts, so the
nature of the words he uses gives
an accurate clue to the type of
mind he possesses.*

—NAPOLEON HILL

Words are the voice of the heart.

—CONFUCIUS

May 12

*Share yourself without expecting a
reward, payment, or commendation.
And above all else keep your
good turn a secret.*
—NAPOLEON HILL

*The greatest pleasure I know,
is to do a good action by stealth,
and have it found out by accident.*
–CHARLES LAMB

May 13

Knowing the Supreme Secret—
what the human mind can believe,
the human mind can achieve—you
see that you have what it takes—
your mind—and you have available
the only other ingredient you
need . . . a world that is bursting
with riches and throbbing with
opportunity.

—NAPOLEON HILL

No great man ever complains
of want of opportunity.

–RALPH WALDO EMERSON

May 14

You can keep your mind trained on that which you desire from Life and get just that! Or you can feed it on the thought of that which you do not desire and it will, as unerringly, bring you just that.

—NAPOLEON HILL

One half of the world must sweat and groan that the other half may dream.
–HENRY WADSWORTH LONGFELLOW

May 15

The man who goes the extra mile and does it in the right kind of "mental attitude" never spends time looking for a job. He does not have to, for the job is always looking for him.

—NAPOLEON HILL

There is no way of making a business successful that can vie with the policy of promoting those who render exceptional service.

—ANDREW CARNEGIE

May 16

The pot of gold at the "end of the rainbow" is not a mere fairy tale! The end of that extra mile is the spot where the rainbow ends, and that is where the pot of gold is hidden.

—NAPOLEON HILL

Good and bad luck is a synonym in the great majority of instances, for good and bad judgment.

–JOHN CHATFIELD

May 17

So-called hunches often are signals indicating that Infinite Intelligence is endeavoring to reach and influence the conscious section of the mind, but you will observe that they usually come in response to some idea, plan, purpose or desire, or some fear that has been handed over to the subconscious section of the mind.

—NAPOLEON HILL

It is only with the heart that one can see rightly; what is essential is invisible to the eye.

—ANTOINE DE SAINT EXUPERY

May 18

Riches which are not shared,
whether they be material riches or
the intangibles, wither and die like
the rose on a severed stem, for it is
one of Nature's first laws that
inaction and disuse lead to decay
and death, and this law applies to
the material possessions of men just
as it applies to the living cells of
every physical body.
—NAPOLEON HILL

Things do not change, we do.
—HENRY DAVID THOREAU

May 19

Do not expect something for nothing. Be willing to give an equivalent value for all that you desire, and include in your plans a definite provision for doing so.

—NAPOLEON HILL

It is the start that stops most people.

–DON SHULA

May 20

Most opinions are worth just what
is asked for them by those who give
them out—nothing!

—NAPOLEON HILL

Every time you give another
a piece of your mind, you add to
your own vacuum.

–FENWICK L. HOLMES

*There are two major occasions
which cause men and women to talk,
and, therefore, advertise favorable or
unfavorably a business; when they
think they have been cheated, and
when they have received fairer
treatment than expected.*
—Napoleon Hill

*Every man takes care that his
neighbor shall not cheat him. But a
day comes when he begins to care
that he does not cheat his neighbor.
Then all goes well.*
–Ralph Waldo Emerson

May 22

Silence is far more effective than words inspired by and mixed with the emotion of anger.

—NAPOLEON HILL

*Only in solitude
do we find ourselves.*

–MIGUEL DE UNAMUNO Y JUGO

May 23

Indecision is the seedling of fear!
—NAPOLEON HILL

*I would rather that my spark
should burn out in a brilliant blaze
than it should be stifled by dry-rot.
I would rather be a superb meteor,
every atom of me in magnificent
glow, than a sleepy and
permanent planet.*
–JACK LONDON

May 24

You can be the master of your fate, the captain of your soul by the simple process of taking possession of your own mind and using it to guide your own life without meddling in the lives of others.
—Napoleon Hill

Shaking off with one mighty effort the fetters of habit, the leaden weight of routine, the cloak of many cares and the slavery of home, man feels once more happy.
–Sir Richard Burton

May 25

*Any idea that is held in the mind,
emphasized, feared or reverenced,
begins at once to clothe itself in the
most convenient and appropriate
physical form that is available.*

—NAPOLEON HILL

*Ideas must work through the
brains and the arms of good and
brave men, or they are no better
than dreams.*

—RALPH WALDO EMERSON

~ Day 145 ~

May 26

Dreams are not born of indifference, laziness, or lack of ambition.

—NAPOLEON HILL

Life is an adventure, dare it.

—MOTHER TERESA

May 27

You must give an equivalent
value for the object of your desire.
Anything you happen to acquire
through sharp practices will have
no enduring value for you.

— NAPOLEON HILL

No person was ever honored for
what he received. Honor has been
the reward for what he gave.

— CALVIN COOLIDGE

May 28

Every mind, or brain, is directly connected with every other brain by means of the ether. Every thought released by any brain may be instantly picked up and interpreted by all other brains that are in rapport with the sending brain.
—NAPOLEON HILL

Thoughts are but dreams till their effect be tried.
–WILLIAM SHAKESPEARE

May 29

Just as the oak tree, in the embryo, sleeps within the acorn, success begins in the form of an intense desire.

—NAPOLEON HILL

Plant the seed of desire in your mind and it forms a nucleus with power to attract to itself everything for its fulfillment.

—ROBERT COLLIER

May 30

Fortunate is the person who has learned that the most certain way to "get" is to first "give" through some sort of useful service.
—NAPOLEON HILL

No one is useless in this world who lightens the burden of it to anyone else.
–CHARLES DICKENS

May 31

The place to begin changing poverty is in the individual mind, and the way to begin is by inspiring the individual to use his mind, to become creative, to render useful service in return for that which he desires.

—NAPOLEON HILL

Nurture your mind with great thoughts. To believe in the heroic makes heroes.

—BENJAMIN DISRAELI

June

The state of mind must be
belief, not mere hope or wish.
Open-mindedness is
essential for belief.

—NAPOLEON HILL

June 1

Nature yields her most profound secrets to the person who is determined to uncover them.

—NAPOLEON HILL

We talk of our mastery of nature, which sounds very grand; but the fact is we respectfully adapt ourselves, first, to her ways.

—CLARENCE DAY

June 2

*The way of success is the way
to action, based upon organized
thinking followed by action,
action, action.*
—NAPOLEON HILL

*The end of all knowledge
should be in virtuous action.*
—PHILIP SYDNEY

June 3

*Ideas are the only assets
which have no fixed values.*

—NAPOLEON HILL

*Money never starts an idea; it
is the idea that starts the money.*

—WILLIAM J. CAMERON

June 4

If you can see an opportunity as quickly as you can see the faults of others, you will soon be rich.
—NAPOLEON HILL

An optimist sees an opportunity in every calamity; a pessimist sees a calamity in every opportunity.
—WINSTON CHURCHILL

June 5

The purpose of all of these principles is primarily to enable you to take possession of the powers of your mind and keep them turned in a positive manner upon the object of your desire.

—NAPOLEON HILL

Immense power is acquired by assuring yourself in your secret reveries that you were born to control affairs.

—ANDREW CARNEGIE

June 6

*The only people you should
get even with are those who have
helped you.*

—NAPOLEON HILL

*Every great man is always
being helped by everybody; for his
gift is to get good out of all things
and all persons.*

–JOHN RUSKIN

June 7

*Things you give to others, through
expression, are the only things you
are able to retain, remember,
or keep for yourself.*
—NAPOLEON HILL

*It is one of the beautiful
compensations of this life that
no one can sincerely try to help
another without helping himself.*
—CHARLES DUDLEY WARNER

June 8

*Work is a liaison office between
our desires and their fulfillments.*
—NAPOLEON HILL

We work to become, not to acquire.
—ELBERT HUBBARD

June 9

True happiness consists not in the possession of things, but in the privilege of self-expression through the use of material things.
—NAPOLEON HILL

Our most valuable possessions are those which can be shared without lessening—those which, when shared, multiply. Our least valuable possessions, on the other hand, are those which, when divided, are diminished.
–WILLIAM H. DANFORTH

June 10

Nothing is ever produced which does not bear many, or all, of the characteristics of its ancestors.
—NAPOLEON HILL

The human mind cannot create anything. It produces nothing until after having been fertilized by experience and meditation; its acquisitions are the germs of its production.
—GEORGE DE BUFFON

June 11

*The conscious mind makes the
plan and decides what shall be
done. The subconscious mind
develops the power to do it.*

—NAPOLEON HILL

*The most fertile soil does not
necessarily produce the most
abundant harvest. It is the use
we make of our faculties which
renders them valuable.*

–THOMAS W. HIGGINSON

June 12

The subconscious mind appears to be the only doorway of individual approach to Infinite Intelligence, and it is capable of being influenced by the individual.

—NAPOLEON HILL

I know this world is ruled by Infinite Intelligence. It required Infinite Intelligence to create it and it requires Infinite Intelligence to keep it on its course. Everything that surrounds us—everything that exists—proves that there are Infinite Laws behind it. There can be no denying this fact. It is mathematical in its precision.

—THOMAS EDISON

June 13

When you have talked yourself
into what you want, right there is
the place to stop talking and begin
saying it with deeds.

—NAPOLEON HILL

The chiefest action for a man of
spirit is never to be out of action;
the soul was never put into the
body to stand still.

—JOHN WEBSTER

June 14

To be an educated man you
must learn how to get what you
want without violating the rights
of others.

—Napoleon Hill

You should have education enough
so that you won't have to look up to
people; and then more education so
that you will be wise enough not to
look down on people.

–M. L. Boren

June 15

No scheme or plan is perfect.
Perfection is a process, not an end.
—Napoleon Hill

Aim at perfection in everything,
though in most things it is
unattainable. However, they who
aim at it, and persevere, will come
much nearer to it than those whose
laziness and despondency make
them give it up as unattainable.
—Lord Chesterfield

June 16

It seems significant that any master mind, to endure, must be based upon justice and fairness to all whom it affects.

—Napoleon Hill

The world must learn to work together, or finally it will not work at all.

—Dwight D. Eisenhower

June 17

Action, or work, is the
connecting link between desire,
plan and fulfillment.
—NAPOLEON HILL

Good actions ennoble us, and we
are the sons of our own deeds.
—MIGUEL DE CERVANTES

June 18

Perhaps the best way faith can be explained is to say that it is man's awareness of, belief in, and harmonizing with the universal powers surrounding him as he feels them.

—NAPOLEON HILL

Faith is raising the sail of our little boat until it is caught up in the soft winds above and picks up speed, not from anything within itself, but from the vast resources of the universe around us.

–W. RALPH WARD, JR.

June 19

Faith is a state of mind which may develop by conditioning your mind to receive Infinite Intelligence.

—Napoleon Hill

Faith is to believe what we do not see; and the reward of this faith is to see what we believe.

—St. Augustine

June 20

Applied faith is the adaptation
of the power received from Infinite
Intelligence to a definite
major purpose.

—Napoleon Hill

A man of courage is also full of faith.

—Cicero

June 21

*Whatever the mind of man
conceives, man can achieve, so long
as his conception does not run
counter to any natural laws and
is in harmony with a moral
and orderly universe.*

—NAPOLEON HILL

*When moral courage feels that it
is in the right, there is no personal
daring of which it is incapable.*

—LEIGH HUNT

June 22

*Whatever we accept, whatever
we love, cherish or desire with a
burning desire and hold constantly
in our thoughts as our own, finds
fulfillment in our lives.*
—NAPOLEON HILL

*Beware of what you
want—for you will get it.*
—RALPH WALDO EMERSON

June 23

If you have faith, keep your mind on that which you want and off that which you do not want.

—NAPOLEON HILL

It seems to me we can never give up longing and wishing while we are thoroughly alive. There are certain things we feel to be beautiful and good, and we must hunger after them.

—GEORGE ELIOT

June 24

*Like the flower which lies latent
in the unopened bud, the seed of
your burning desire needs only the
sunshine and moisture of your
faith to start germinating.*
—NAPOLEON HILL

*True effort, in fact, as of a
captive struggling to free himself:
That is thought.*
—THOMAS CARLYLE

June 25

When the plan comes through to
your conscious mind, accept it with
appreciation and gratitude—and
act on it at once.

—NAPOLEON HILL

An intelligent plan is
the first step to success.

—BASIL S. WALSH

June 26

*If you will make your prayers
an expression of gratitude and
thanksgiving for the blessings you
have already received, instead of
requests for what you do not
have, you will obtain results a
great deal faster.*

—NAPOLEON HILL

*The worship most acceptable
to God comes from a thankful
and cheerful heart.*

—PLUTARCH

June 27

The difference between success and failure is largely a matter of the difference between positive and negative thought. A negative mind will not attract a fortune. Like attracts like. Nothing attracts success as quickly as success.
—NAPOLEON HILL

No pessimist ever discovered the secret of the stars, or sailed to an uncharted land, or opened a new doorway to the human spirit.
—HELEN KELLER

June 28

Be sure that your desires tend
toward giving and good. It is hard
to make a snowball by pushing it
up the hill, counter to the natural
law of life. If you try, you will find
that it will become bigger than you
and get out of control.

—NAPOLEON HILL

Happy the man who early learns
the wide chasm that lies between
his wishes and his powers!

—JOHANN WOLFGANG VON GOETHE

June 29

The law of attraction is based upon the principle of growth from the vitality which is inherent in the seed (idea or desire) itself. Every seed has, in itself, a potentially perfect plant. Every worthy desire has in it the potential for its perfect fulfillment.

—NAPOLEON HILL

Ideas are the roots of creation.

—ERNEST DIMNET

June 30

The power of thought produces astounding results when the law of cosmic habitforce takes over the thought pattern and carries it out automatically.

—NAPOLEON HILL

No seed shall perish
which the soul hath sown.

–JOHN ADDINGTON SYMONDS

July

Defeat may be a stepping-
stone or a stumbling block
depending on whether your
attitude is positive or
negative.

—Napoleon Hill

July 1

Motivation is that which induces action or determines choice. It is the hope or other force which starts an action in an attempt to produce specific results.

—NAPOLEON HILL

Cause and effect, means and ends, seed and fruit cannot be severed; for the effect already blooms in the cause, the end preexists in the means, the fruit in the seed.

—RALPH WALDO EMERSON

~ Day 182 ~

July 2

Hope is the magic ingredient
in motivating yourself and others.
—NAPOLEON HILL

Hope: Desire and
expectation rolled into one.
—AMBROSE BIERCE

July 3

Remember, the thoughts that you think and the statements you make regarding yourself determine your mental attitude. If you have a worthwhile objective, find the one reason why you can achieve it rather than hundreds of reasons why you can't.

—NAPOLEON HILL

Science may have found a cure for most evils; but it has found no remedy for the worst of them all— the apathy of human beings.

—HELEN KELLER

~ Day 184 ~

July 4

As the compass of a ship is affected by disturbing magnetic influences, requiring the pilot to make certain allowances in order to keep the vessel on its right course, so you must take account of the powerful influences affecting you as you navigate through life.

—NAPOLEON HILL

It is interesting to notice how some minds seem almost to create themselves, springing up under every disadvantage and working their solitary but irresistible way through a thousand obstacles.

—WASHINGTON IRVING

July 5

The important fact to remember is that self-discipline calls for a balancing of the emotions of your heart with the reasoning faculty of your mind.

—NAPOLEON HILL

The appearance of things change according to the emotions and thus we see magic and beauty in them, while the magic and beauty are really in ourselves.

–KAHLIL GIBRAN

~ Day 186 ~

July 6

Success in all the higher
brackets of individual achievement
is reached by the application of
thought-power, properly organized,
concentrated and directed toward
definite ends. Any power, thought
or physical, is achieved by
concentration of energy!
—NAPOLEON HILL

A man doesn't need brilliance
or genius, all he needs is energy.
—ALBERT M. GREENFIELD

July 7

*Our body, for example, is
one of nature's most remarkable
demonstrations of the power
and the value of team work.*
—NAPOLEON HILL

*Our body is a well-set clock,
which keeps good time, but if
it be too much or indiscreetly
tampered with, the alarm runs
out before the hour.*
—JOSEPH HALL

~ Day 188 ~

July 8

The man with creative vision knows that he can succeed only by helping others succeed, and he knows also that it is not necessary for another man to fail in order that he may succeed.

—NAPOLEON HILL

If there is any great secret of success in life, it lies in the ability to put yourself in the other person's place and to see things from his point of view—as well as your own.

–HENRY FORD

July 9

Nature has no free hand-outs for anything, or anyone. But the birds of the air alternate between their search for food, and their joy in song.

—NAPOLEON HILL

To preserve their independence, we must not let our rules load us with perpetual debt. We must make our election between economy and liberty, or profusion and servitude.

—THOMAS JEFFERSON

July 10

Nobody who goes too deeply
into debt can count on having
peace of mind.

—NAPOLEON HILL

Debt is slavery of the free.

—PUBLILIUS SYRUS

July 11

Ideas are intangible forces, but
they have more power than the
physical brains that give birth to
them. They have the power to live
on, after the brain that creates them
has returned to dust.

—NAPOLEON HILL

There is one thing stronger than all
the armies in the world, and that is
an idea whose time has come.

—VICTOR HUGO

~ Day 192 ~

July 12

What is the only permanent state
of affairs throughout the universe?
It is change—eternal change—as
nature forever builds, evolves, tears
down, rebuilds in an ever-onward
march toward some destiny
unknown to man.

—NAPOLEON HILL

All things change, and you
yourself are constantly wasting
away. So also is the universe.

–MARCUS AURELIUS ANTONINUS

July 13

*Be wealthy in your own way
and you will know that you are
wealthy . . . and bear in mind that
even a beggar enjoys the beauty of
the earth, the drift of white clouds
and the sight of a rainbow or a
twinkling star.*

—NAPOLEON HILL

*Wealth is not only what you
have but it is also what you are.*

—STERLING W. SILL

~ Day 194 ~

July 14

Giving begets receiving: there is a to-and-fro passage of wealth which may not reflect itself in a swollen bank account, but does reflect itself in a mind which has known such wealth. In this lies happiness, peace and health which a man merely rich in money may never know.

—Napoleon Hill

If a rich man is proud of his wealth, he should not be praised until it is known how he employs it.

—Socrates

July 15

A mind at peace is a mind that is free to conceive greatly. It bears no great conflicts within its subconscious which may hamper the conscious mind and therefore conscious action. A mind at peace is a free mind. Its power is limitless.

—NAPOLEON HILL

Calmness of mind is one of the beautiful jewels of wisdom. It is the result of long and patient effort in self-control. Its presence is an indication of ripened experience and of a more than ordinary knowledge of the laws and operations of thought.

—JAMES ALLEN

~ Day 196 ~

July 16

*It has been said that if you can
make a man laugh, you can make
him like you. If he likes you, he will
also listen to what you have to say
in a serious vein.*

—NAPOLEON HILL

*Men will let you abuse them
if only you will make them laugh.*

–HENRY WARD BEECHER

July 17

Every act, situation, or choice of our lives contains cause and effect. In adversities we have situations in which we are made very much aware of the effect.

—Napoleon Hill

Choose always the way that seems the best, however rough it may be; custom will soon render it easy and agreeable.

—Pythagoras

July 18

If you have your mental attitude under control you may control almost all other circumstances which affect your life, including your fears and worries of every nature whatsoever.

—NAPOLEON HILL

Peace of mind: The contentment of the man who is too busy to worry by day, and too sleepy to worry at night.

—WOODROW WILSON

July 19

Truly, we may become the captains of our worldly destiny precisely to the extent that we take possession of our own minds and direct them to definite ends through control of our mental attitude.

—NAPOLEON HILL

Most of the critical things in life, which become the starting points of human destiny, are little things.

–R. SMITH

~ *Day 200* ~

July 20

Fear, in any form, is not only the major stumbling block which brings failure in connection with one's calling, but fear is also the major reason why most prayers bring only negative results.

—NAPOLEON HILL

If fear is cultivated it will become stronger. If faith is cultivated it will achieve the mastery. We have a right to believe that faith is the stronger emotion because it is positive whereas fear is negative.

–JOHN PAUL JONES

~ Day 201 ~

July 21

Strength, both physical and spiritual, is the product of struggle!
—Napoleon Hill

Know how sublime a thing it is to suffer and be strong.
–Henry Wadsworth Longfellow

~ Day 202 ~

July 22

No man has a chance to enjoy
permanent success until he begins
to look in a mirror for the real
cause of all his mistakes.

—NAPOLEON HILL

People will listen a great deal
more patiently when you explain
your mistakes than when you
explain your success.

–WILBUR D. NESBIT

July 23

Service, Sacrifice and Self-Control are three words which must be well understood by the person who succeeds in doing something that is of help to the world.

—NAPOLEON HILL

The race of mankind would perish did they cease to aid each other. We cannot exist without mutual help. All therefore that need aid have a right to ask it from their fellow-men; and no one who has the power of granting can refuse it without guilt.

–SIR WALTER SCOTT

July 24

Aspiration is greater than realization, because it keeps us eternally climbing upward toward some unattained goal.

—Napoleon Hill

Far away there in the sunshine are my highest aspirations. I may not reach them, but I can look up and see their beauty, believe in them and try to follow where they lead.

—Louisa May Alcott

July 25

Great personal power is
acquired only through the
harmonious cooperation of a
number of people who concentrate
their efforts upon some
definite plan.

—NAPOLEON HILL

In a balanced organization,
working towards a common
objective, there is success.

—T. L. SCRUTTON

July 26

*Power (man power) is
organized knowledge, expressed
through intelligent action!*
—Napoleon Hill

*Every great advance in natural
knowledge has involved the
absolute rejection of authority.*
—Thomas H. Huxley

July 27

The health of the body as well as the mind, is literally built upon the principle of harmony! The energy known as life begins to disintegrate and death approaches when the organs of the body stop working in harmony.

—Napoleon Hill

True enjoyment comes from activity of the mind and exercise of the body; the two are united.

—Alexander von Humboldt

~ Day 208 ~

July 28

*Enthusiasm is simply a high
rate of vibration of the mind.*
—NAPOLEON HILL

*Every production of genius must
be the production of enthusiasm.*
—BENJAMIN DISRAELI

July 29

Not one single successful person was discovered whose success was attained without the experience of what, in many instances, seemed like unbearable obstacles that had to be mastered.

—NAPOLEON HILL

You never will be the person you can be if pressure, tension and discipline are taken out of your life.

—JAMES G. BILKEY

July 30

Everything that any man ever created or built was first visioned, in his own mind, through imagination.

—NAPOLEON HILL

The man who will use his skill and constructive imagination to see how much he can give for a dollar, instead of how little he can give for a dollar, is bound to succeed.

–HENRY FORD

~ Day 211 ~

July 31

Plain, unemotional words do not
influence the subconscious mind.
You will get no appreciable results
until you learn to reach your
subconscious mind with thoughts,
or spoken words which have been
well emotionalized with belief.

—NAPOLEON HILL

Our emotions are the driving
powers of our lives. When we are
aroused emotionally, unless we do
something great and good, we are in
danger of letting our emotions
become perverted.

—EARL RINEY

August

If you set a goal, you are more apt to recognize things that will help you achieve it than if you don't set a goal.

—Napoleon Hill

August 1

*Somewhere in the cell-structure of
the brain is located an organ which
receives vibrations of thought
ordinarily called "hunches."*
—NAPOLEON HILL

*Intuition is perception
via the unconscious.*
—CARL JUNG

August 2

The successful leader of the future, whether in the field of selling or in other walks of life, must make the golden rule the basis of his leadership.

—NAPOLEON HILL

Kindness can become its own motive. We are made kind by being kind.

–ERIC HOFFER

August 3

Every human being is ruled by the law of habit. Because this is true, the person who learns to build his habits to order practically controls the major cause of successful achievement.

—Napoleon Hill

The great pleasure in life is doing what people say you cannot do.

—Walter Bagehot

August 4

Successful men never wait for others to show them what to do or how to do it.

—NAPOLEON HILL

We have forty million reasons for failure, but not a single excuse.

—RUDYARD KIPLING

August 5

---

*Nothing builds confidence
more quickly than a keen, genuine
interest in the buyer's business
problems.*

—NAPOLEON HILL

Self-assurance reassures others.

–GARRY WILLS

August 6

*Words, woven into combinations
of thought which create desire,
will sell.*

—NAPOLEON HILL

*Words—so innocent and
powerless as they are, as
standing in a dictionary, how
potent for good and evil they
become, in the hands of one who
knows how to combine them!*

—NATHANIEL HAWTHORNE

August 7

If you are successful remember that somewhere, sometime, someone gave you a lift or an idea that started you in the right direction.

—NAPOLEON HILL

The spirit of brotherhood recognizes of necessity both the need of self-help and also the need of helping others in the only way which ever ultimately does great good, that is, of helping them to help themselves.

—THEODORE ROOSEVELT

~ Day 219 ~

August 8

*Remember, also, that you are
indebted to life until you help some
less fortunate person, just as you
were helped.*

—NAPOLEON HILL

*It is great to be great, but
it is greater to be human.*

–WILL ROGERS

August 9

Your position is nothing more than your opportunity to show what sort of ability you have. You will get out of it exactly what you put into it— no more and no less.

—NAPOLEON HILL

The workman is known by his work.

—LA FONTAINE

August 10

A "big" position is but the sum
total of numerous "little" positions
well filled.

—NAPOLEON HILL

Words without actions are
the assassins of idealism.

—HERBERT HOOVER

August 11

Those who wait for all the equipment needed before making a start never experience success, because complete equipment is seldom available in the beginning of any person's plans.

—NAPOLEON HILL

Eighty percent of success is showing up.

—WOODY ALLEN

August 12

*Lose yourself in unselfish service
to others and thereby discover the
Master Key to that power from
within which guides one,
unerringly, to the attainment of
one's noblest aims and purposes.*
—NAPOLEON HILL

*If we worry too much about
ourselves, we won't have time
for others.*
—MOTHER TERESA

August 13

The records of successful men of all periods of civilization are replete with evidence that those who attain permanent success always carry others along with them.

—NAPOLEON HILL

The more you establish parameters and encourage people to take initiatives within those boundaries, the more you multiply your own effectiveness by the effectiveness of other people.

—ROBERT HASS

August 14

*The merchant who abuses the
privileges of his customers soon
pays by the loss of his trade.*

—NAPOLEON HILL

*The dignity of every
occupation wholly depends upon
the quantity and the kind of virtue
that may be exerted in it.*

–EDMUND BURKE

August 15

*Decide now what you desire
from life and what you have to
give in return.*

−NAPOLEON HILL

*No one can give you
better advice than yourself.*

−CICERO

August 16

Decide where you are going
and how you are to get there. Then
make a start from where you
now stand.

—NAPOLEON HILL

It is the greatest of all mistakes to
do nothing because you can only do
a little. Do what you can.

—SYDNEY SMITH

~ Day 228 ~

August 17

Make the start with whatever
means of attaining your goal that
may be at hand. And you will
discover that to the extent you make
use of these, other and better means
will reveal themselves to you.

—NAPOLEON HILL

God gives every bird his food, but
He does not throw it into the nest.

–JOSIAH GILBERT HOLLAND

August 18

*Faith begins with definiteness
of purpose functioning in a mind
that has been prepared for it by
the development of a positive
mental attitude.*

—NAPOLEON HILL

*Doubt whom you will,
but never yourself.*

—CHRISTIAN BOVEE

August 19

When PMA (positive mental attitude) takes over, success is just around the corner and defeat is nothing more than an experience with which one may motivate himself for greater effort.
—NAPOLEON HILL

There is only one success—to be able to spend your life in your own way.
—CHRISTOPHER MORLEY

~ Day 231 ~

August 20

Cosmic Habitforce is the medium by
which every living thing is forced to
take on and become a part of the
environmental influences in which
it lives and moves.

—NAPOLEON HILL

*Nature's rules . . .
have no exceptions.*
–HERBERT SPENCER

August 21

The overall purpose of the philosophy is to enable one to get from where he stands to where he wishes to be, both economically and spiritually; thus it prepares one to enjoy the abundant life which the Creator intended all people to enjoy.

—NAPOLEON HILL

The purpose of life is not to be happy—but to matter, to be productive, to be useful, to have it make a difference that you lived at all.

—LEO ROSTEN

~ Day 233 ~

August 22

All thought (whether it is positive or negative, good or bad, accurate or inaccurate) tends to clothe itself in its physical equivalent, and it does so by inspiring one with ideas, plans, and the means of attaining desired ends, through logical and natural means.

—NAPOLEON HILL

The more profound the thought, the more burdensome. What is in will out.

—RALPH WALDO EMERSON

August 23

A person without enthusiasm is
like a watch without a mainspring.
—NAPOLEON HILL

Enthusiasm is of the greatest
value, so long as we are not
carried away by it.
–JOHANN VON GOETHE

August 24

Deeds, not mere words.
                    —NAPOLEON HILL

*Self-knowledge is best learned, not
by contemplation, but action. Strive
to do your duty, and you will soon
discover of what stuff you are
made.*
                    —JOHANN VON GOETHE

August 25

*When you share with others a
part of what you have, that which
remains will multiply and grow.*

—NAPOLEON HILL

*The more we share,
the more we have.*

—LEONARD NIMOY

August 26

Education comes from within;
you get it by struggle and effort
and thought.

—NAPOLEON HILL

The aim of all education is,
or should be, to teach people to
educate themselves.

–ARNOLD J. TOYNBEE

August 27

There is power in the spoken
word . . . avoid all-inclusive,
restrictive words such as never,
only, nothing, every, everyone,
no one and can't.

—NAPOLEON HILL

Words are . . . the most
powerful drug used by mankind.

–RUDYARD KIPLING

August 28

Do not settle for anything
short of what you want.
—NAPOLEON HILL

It's never too late to be
what you might have been.
—GEORGE ELIOT

August 29

*Close the door of fear behind
you, and see how quickly the door
to success opens in front of you.*
—NAPOLEON HILL

*The old skin has to be shed
before the new one can come.*
—JOSEPH CAMPBELL

~ Day 241 ~

August 30

*Ability is more valuable than
money because it can be neither
lost nor stolen.*

—NAPOLEON HILL

*The wise man will make
more opportunities than he finds.*

–SIR FRANCIS BACON

August 31

*The mind grows only through
use; it atrophies through idleness.*
—Napoleon Hill

*When love and skill work
together, expect a masterpiece.*
—John Ruskin

September

*Keep your conscious
mind focused on what you
want, and your subconscious
mind will unerringly
guide you to it.*

—NAPOLEON HILL

September 1

*A man's ego is his greatest asset
or his greatest liability, according
to the way in which he relates
himself to it.*

—NAPOLEON HILL

*The World is a great mirror.
It reflects back to you what you are.
If you are loving, if you are friendly,
if you are helpful, the World will
prove loving and friendly and
helpful to you. The World is
what you are.*

—THOMAS DRIER

September 2

All voluntary positive habits
are the products of will power
directed toward the attainment
of definite goals.

—NAPOLEON HILL

You must respect the things in
life that you want to attract.

—MIKE MURDOCK

September 3

*Your measure of respect for time
is opportunity's measure of respect
for you.*

—Napoleon Hill

*He who has begun,
has the work half done.*

—Horace

September 4

*The man of decision cannot be
stopped! The man of indecision
cannot be started!*

—NAPOLEON HILL

*Your sole contribution to
the sum of things is yourself.*

—FRANK CRANE

September 5

*We have only to conceive
the idea and believe the idea
to achieve the idea.*

—Napoleon Hill

*There is no fate that plans men's
lives. Whatever comes to us, good
or bad, is usually the result of our
own action or lack of action.*

–Herbert N. Casson

~ Day 248 ~

September 6

*Be as careful of the thought
you mix with your food as you
are in the choice of food itself.*
—NAPOLEON HILL

*The purpose of life, after all, is
to live it, to taste experience to the
utmost, to reach out eagerly and
without fear for newer and
richer experience.*
—ELEANOR ROOSEVELT

~ Day 249 ~

September 7

*Creative vision may be an
inborn quality of the mind, or
it may be an acquired quality, for
it may be developed by the free
and fearless use of the faculty
of the imagination.*

—NAPOLEON HILL

Wisdom begins in wonder.

—SOCRATES

September 8

Creative vision has its base in the spirit of the universe which expresses itself through the brain of man.

—NAPOLEON HILL

Somewhere up above, there is a universal guidance system, and you are on that radar screen.

—SQUIRE RUSHNELL

~ Day 251 ~

September 9

Success without humility of heart
is apt to prove only temporary and
unsatisfying.

—NAPOLEON HILL

If you have knowledge, let
others light their candles at it.

—MARGARET FULLER

September 10

*A positive mental attitude is
an essential part of the key which
unlocks the door to the solution
of all personal problems.*

—NAPOLEON HILL

*Beginning today, treat everyone
you meet as if they were going to
be dead by midnight. Extend to them
all the care, kindness, and understanding
you can muster, and do it with no
thought of any reward. Your life
will never be the same again.*

–OG MANDINO

September 11

*Until we become inspired with
this broad spirit of team work, and
recognize the oneness of all people
and the fellowship of all mankind, we
will not be in a position to benefit by
the principle of cooperative effort.
Greed and selfishness have no
part in this spirit.*

—NAPOLEON HILL

*We must indeed all hang
together, or most assuredly we
will all hang separately.*

–BENJAMIN FRANKLIN

~ Day 254 ~

September 12

*Team work differs from the
master mind principle in that it
is based on coordination of effort
without necessarily embracing the
principle of definiteness of purpose
or the principle of absolute
harmony, two important essentials
of the master mind.*
—NAPOLEON HILL

*We build too many walls
and not enough bridges.*
–SIR ISAAC NEWTON

~ Day 255 ~

September 13

Your mind is never idle. It works all the time. It's up to you to put it to work producing the things you want, rather than letting it run wild, attracting things you don't want.

—NAPOLEON HILL

Our best friends and our worst enemies are our thoughts. A thought can do us more good than a doctor or a banker or a faithful friend. It can also do us more harm than a brick.

—FRANK CRANE

September 14

*Remember, it is not necessary
for others to fail in order that you
may succeed.*

—Napoleon Hill

*Nature is an inexhaustible
storehouse of riches; the supply
will never run short.*

—Wallace D. Wattles

September 15

Thoughts are things, and it is significant that thought is the only power over which any individual has been provided, by the Creator of man, with the right of complete control.

—NAPOLEON HILL

Our thought can bring out a condition as perfect as we can conceive.

–ERNEST HOLMES

~ Day 258 ~

September 16

Next to life itself, the greatest miracle known to man is the miracle of thought, and no small part of this miracle consists in the amazing simplicity with which so complicated a mechanism as the brain can be operated by the power of will.

—NAPOLEON HILL

A thought,—good or evil,—an act in time a habit,—so runs life's law; what you live in your thought-world that sooner or later you will find objectified in your life.

–RALPH WALDO TRINE

September 17

*Self-discipline is the tool
with which man may harness
and direct his inborn emotions in
the direction of his choice.*

—NAPOLEON HILL

*Self-conquest is the
greatest of victories.*

—PLATO

September 18

One peculiar characteristic of
the subconscious mind is that it
will not take orders from the
conscious mind. It acts only upon
order of the emotions.

—NAPOLEON HILL

When your emotional nature
is stirred by something you do, is
it not probable that your heart is
actually stimulated, so that it
quickens the circulation of your
blood and makes you feel alive
and full of health?

–DAVID DUNN

September 19

*Enthusiasm bears the same
relationship to a human being
that fire bears to a steam boiler. It
concentrates the powers of the mind
and gives them the wings of action.*
—NAPOLEON HILL

*Start by doing what's necessary,
then what's possible and suddenly
you are doing the impossible.*
—FRANCIS OF ASSISI

September 20

*Enthusiasm is a great leavening
force in your mental world, for it
gives power to your purpose.*
—NAPOLEON HILL

*The men who do the most with
their lives are those who approach
human existence, its opportunities
and its problems—even in rough
moments—with a confident attitude
and an enthusiastic point of view.*
—NORMAN VINCENT PEALE

~ Day 263 ~

September 21

*A positive mind finds a way it
can be done, a negative mind looks
for all the ways it can't be done.*

—NAPOLEON HILL

*You can come out of the furnace
of trouble two ways: if you let it
consume you, you come out a cinder;
but there is a kind of mental which
refuses to be consumed, and
comes out a star.*

—JEAN CHURCH

~ Day 264 ~

September 22

*When you close the door of your
mind to negative thoughts, the door
of opportunity opens to you.*
—NAPOLEON HILL

*You can struggle all your life
without making much progress—
when suddenly a single idea can
lift you out of obscurity into the
limelight of success and happiness.*
–BEN SWEETLAND

September 23

The mind that has been made to receive, attracts that which it needs, just as a magnet attracts steel fillings.

—NAPOLEON HILL

You are the sum total of all the causes and effects you have set up in yourself through your mental and emotional attitudes. Their end result is the you that you are right this minute!

—CLAUDE M. BRISTOL

~ Day 266 ~

September 24

Every time you stumble and fall,
but rise again, you learn wisdom.
Wisdom comes from failure much
more than from success.
—NAPOLEON HILL

Failure is success if we learn from it.
—MALCOLM FORBES

September 25

Humility of heart is the outgrowth of understanding of man's relationship to his Creator, plus the recognition of the fact that all the material blessings of life are gifts from the Creator for the common good of all mankind.

—NAPOLEON HILL

It is not in a man's creed but in his deeds, not in his knowledge but in his wisdom, not in his power, but in his sympathy that there lies the essence of what is good and what will last in human life.

—F. YORKE POWELL

September 26

Temperance in all things and over-indulgence in none should be the motto of every person seeking to develop an attractive personality.

—NAPOLEON HILL

A man who trims himself to suit everybody will soon whittle himself away.

–CHARLES M. SCHWAB

September 27

*The tolerant person keeps his
mind open to receive new and
different facts and knowledge
on all subjects.*

—Napoleon Hill

*It is better to correct your
own faults than those of another.*

—Democritus

September 28

*Life is one continuous series
of experiences in salesmanship
through which one must sell himself
to every person he meets in his
social, professional or
occupational contacts.*
—NAPOLEON HILL

*We didn't all come over on the same
ship, but we're all in the same boat.*
—BERNARD M. BARUCH

~ Day 271 ~

September 29

You require no one's permission
to . . . go the extra mile. The person
who renders the greatest service
also uncovers the greatest
opportunities for self-benefit.
—NAPOLEON HILL

All the beautiful sentiments
in the world weigh less than a
simple lovely action.
—JAMES RUSSELL LOWELL

September 30

*That which you think today
becomes that which you are
tomorrow.*
—NAPOLEON HILL

*Important principles
may and must be inflexible.*
—ABRAHAM LINCOLN

October

Render more and better service than is expected of you if you wish to achieve success.

—Napoleon Hill

October 1

The conscious mind is the architect; the subconscious mind is the vast storehouse from which may be requisitioned the mental materials for the project which is under construction.

—NAPOLEON HILL

Nothing splendid has ever been achieved except by those who dared believe that something inside them was superior to circumstance.

—BRUCE BARTON

October 2

Concentration on one's major purpose projects a clear picture of that purpose upon the conscious mind and holds it there until it is taken over by the subconscious and acted upon.
—Napoleon Hill

I have learned through bitter experience the one supreme lesson: to conserve my anger, and as heat conserved is transmitted into energy, even so our anger controlled can be transmitted into a power that can move the world.
—Mahatma Gandhi

~ Day 275 ~

October 3

There are people in this world
who have nothing better to do than
stand on the side lines of life and
stick out their feet just to see others
tumble, and if they learn which
way you're going, they may be
lying in wait for you.

—NAPOLEON HILL

Where you stumble,
there your treasure lies.

—JOSEPH CAMPBELL

~ Day 276 ~

October 4

*The mind has been provided with
a gateway of approach to Infinite
Intelligence through what is known
as the subconscious mind.*
—NAPOLEON HILL

*I steer my bark with
Hope ahead and Fear astern.*
–THOMAS JEFFERSON

October 5

*From the vast reservoir of Infinite
Intelligence, through the gateway of
the subconscious mind, there flows
into the conscious mind of man a
continual stream of intelligence
upon which we are dependent for
our growth and development, and
the unfolding of our innate powers.*
—NAPOLEON HILL

*Let nothing disturb thee,
Nothing affright thee.
All things are passing—
God never changeth.*
—H. W. LONGFELLOW

October 6

*Successful men do not
bargain with life for poverty!*
—NAPOLEON HILL

*Worry or resentment allowed to
grow within yourself is almost like
signing your own death certificate
in advance.*
—WALTER M. GERMAIN

October 7

*The foreman who has flexibility
will have the fullest cooperation of
all of his men, because he will relate
himself to each man according to
that man's personality.*
—NAPOLEON HILL

*It is no use walking anywhere
to preach unless our walking is
our preaching.*
–ST. FRANCIS OF ASSISI

October 8

There are two things which nature
discourages and severely penalizes:
(a) a vacuum (emptiness) and (b)
idleness (lack of action).
—NAPOLEON HILL

To drift is to be in hell;
To be in heaven is to steer.
—GEORGE BERNARD SHAW

October 9

*At birth each of us figuratively
brings with him two sealed
envelopes: one is labeled Rewards,
and the other Penalties.*
—NAPOLEON HILL

*We don't know who we are
until we see what we can do.*
—MARTHA GRIMES

October 10

You either use your brain for
controlled thinking in connection
with things you want, or nature
steps in and uses it to grow a crop
of negative circumstances you do
not want.

—NAPOLEON HILL

It's the start that stops most people.

–DON SHULA

October 11

You can take possession of your thought power, or you can let it be influenced by the stray winds of chance and circumstances you do not desire.

—NAPOLEON HILL

Our aspirations are our possibilities.

—ROBERT BROWNING

October 12

You can always become the
person you would have liked to be.
—NAPOLEON HILL

Great things are not done by
impulse, but by a series of small
things brought together.
—VINCENT VAN GOGH

October 13

*A positive mental attitude is a
'must' for all who wish to make life
pay off on their own terms.*
—Napoleon Hill

*Winning is a habit.
Unfortunately, so is losing.*
—Vince Lombardi

October 14

*If you have objectionable habits
which you wish to break, show
yourself who is boss by abstaining
from such habits for one month.*
—NAPOLEON HILL

*Genius is only the power
of making continuous effort.*
–ELBERT HUBBARD

October 15

*Keep a daily diary of your good
deeds in behalf of others, and never
let the sun set on a single day
without recording some act of
human kindness.*

—NAPOLEON HILL

*When I do good, I feel good.
When I do bad, I feel bad.
And that's my religion.*

–ABRAHAM LINCOLN

October 16

*For every favor or benefit
you receive give an equal benefit
to others.*

—NAPOLEON HILL

*The winds of grace are always
blowing. It is you that must raise
your sails.*

–RABINDRANATH TAGORE

October 17

*Learn the difference
between wishing, hoping, desiring
and—having a burning desire to
achieve your purposes in life.*
—NAPOLEON HILL

*Do not grasp at the stars, but
do life's plain common work as it
comes, certain that daily duties
and daily bread are the
sweetest things of life.*
—LORD HOUGHTON

October 18

A burning desire is a driving, motivating force which is more compelling than wishing, hoping and ordinary desires all rolled into one.

—NAPOLEON HILL

In the depth of winter, I finally learned that there was in me an invincible summer.

–ALBERT CAMUS

~ Day 291 ~

October 19

A burning desire can be kept alive only by the aid of a positive mental attitude.

—NAPOLEON HILL

It is not light that we need but fire; it is not the gentle shower, but thunder. We need the storm, the whirlwind, and the earthquake.

—FREDERICK DOUGLASS

October 20

Be careful of your associates
because the negative mental attitude
of other people is very contagious
and it rubs off on one a little
at a time.

—NAPOLEON HILL

Everyone is a moon and has
a dark side which he never shows
to anybody.

–MARK TWAIN

October 21

Enthusiasm will not mix with fear, envy, greed, jealousy, doubt, revenge, hatred, intolerance and procrastination.
—NAPOLEON HILL

No man ever choked to death swallowing his own pride.
—RALPH W. SOCKMAN

~ Day 294 ~

October 22

*Enthusiasm thrives only on
positive thought and action.*
—NAPOLEON HILL

*Enthusiasm is the yeast that
makes your hopes rise to the stars.
Enthusiasm is the sparkle in
your eyes, the swing in your gait,
the grip of your hand,
the irresistible surge of will
and energy to execute your ideas.*
–HENRY FORD

~ Day 295 ~

October 23

One of the strange effects of a master mind alliance is the fact that it brings into operation the principle of increasing returns by stepping up vibrations of thought, thus leading to the state of mind known as faith.

—NAPOLEON HILL

If it can be verified, we don't need faith . . . . Faith is for that which lies on the other side of reason. Faith is what makes life bearable, with all its tragedies and ambiguities and sudden, startling joys.

—MADELEINE L 'ENGLE

October 24

On the whole, more men survive
the test of defeat than survive the
test of success, for experience
proves that power, fame and
material riches, especially if they
come too easily or too quickly, often
lead to one's undoing.
—NAPOLEON HILL

The worst bankrupt in the
world is the man who has lost his
enthusiasm. Let a man lose
everything else in the world but his
enthusiasm and he will come
through again to success.
–H. W. ARNOLD

October 25

Every man is his brother's keeper,
whether he chooses to recognize this
fact or not. And there is always a
far greater degree of benefit to
those who serve than to those
who merely receive.

—NAPOLEON HILL

Real joy comes not from ease
or riches or from the praise of men,
but from doing something
worthwhile.

—SIR WILFRED GRENFELL

October 26

A keen sense of humor, no
matter how it is indulged,
provides relaxation.

—NAPOLEON HILL

If you want to lift yourself
up, lift up someone else.

—BOOKER T. WASHINGTON

October 27

Nothing about life is static or unchanging. There seems to be a constant wave-like motion to life.
—NAPOLEON HILL

Each of us is given a heritage and a legacy the moment we come into this world: talents, time, life. What we do with these possessions, how we invest them, determines what we are.
—MARCUS BACH

~ Day 300 ~

October 28

Work is a great blessing only when it is performed in the right mental attitude, as a labor of love.

—Napoleon Hill

Your effectiveness as a person can be measured by your ability to complete things. Incomplete and unresolved elements of life drain our resources and waste our creative energy.

—Dr. Robert Anthony

October 29

Mental suffering, in times of great emergency, provides a mind stimulant of stupendous proportions. Mutual suffering has the effect of causing people to consolidate their mind power, through the mastermind principle, and direct it to the alleviation of their suffering.

—NAPOLEON HILL

I not only use all the brains I have but all I can borrow.

—WOODROW WILSON

~ Day 302 ~

October 30

*There is something about
the uncertainty of time which is
awe-inspiring, for time is the one
great asset which cannot be bought
and cannot be prolonged by the
mere desire to live.*

—NAPOLEON HILL

*One of the most tragic things I know
about human nature is that all of us
tend to put off living. We are all
dreaming of some magical rose
garden over the horizon—instead of
enjoying the roses that are blooming
outside our windows today.*

–DALE CARNEGIE

October 31

---

*The great leaders of the world
always have been men of decision
who had a high respect for time.*
—NAPOLEON HILL

*You cannot dream yourself into
a character; you must hammer and
forge yourself one.*
—JAMES A. FROUDE

November

If you're unhappy with your world and want to change it, the place to begin is with yourself.

—NAPOLEON HILL

November 1

*Faith is the state of mind wherein
you temporarily relax your own
reason and will power, and open
your mind completely to the inflow
of power from Infinite Intelligence.*
—NAPOLEON HILL

*Faith may be defined briefly
as an illogical belief in the
occurrence of the improbable.*
–H. L. MENCKEN

November 2

Through the application of the master mind principle, you can increase the acreage of your fertile soil and thus produce a bigger crop.

—NAPOLEON HILL

What prodigious power a large body of men can put forth when they all work at the same task and are greatly interested in it. They begin by the same process, but the process differentiates and improves in their hands. Each gains skill and dexterity. They learn from each other, and the product is multiplied.

—WILLIAM GRAHAM SUMNER

November 3

The law of attraction is based upon the principle of growth from the vitality which is inherent in the seed (idea or desire) itself.

—NAPOLEON HILL

*A man there was
they called him mad.
The more he gave
the more he had.*

—JOHN BUNYAN

November 4

Every seed has, in itself,
a potentially perfect plant.
— NAPOLEON HILL

Whatever you are by nature,
keep to it; never desert your line
of talent. Be what nature intended
you for, and you will succeed.
— SYDNEY SMITH

November 5

Every worthy desire has in it the potential power for its perfect fulfillment.

—NAPOLEON HILL

I always prefer to believe the best of everybody—it saves so much trouble.

—RUDYARD KIPLING

November 6

If a seed is to germinate and produce a crop after its own kind, it must be planted in fertile soil, it must have nourishment, and it must have sunshine to ripen it for harvest.

—NAPOLEON HILL

Growth is the only evidence of life.

—CARDINAL NEWMAN

November 7

Your subconscious mind can be
compared to a fertile garden spot
wherein may be planted the seed of
your definite purpose, by means of
a burning desire which imparts the
initial energy into the nucleus of
your definite purpose, and causes
it to enlarge and grow.

—NAPOLEON HILL

All that we are
arises with our thoughts.

—BUDDHA

~ Day 311 ~

November 8

The analogy of planting and growing is to impress you with the possibility of employing the powers of your own mind, coupled with and activated by the power of Infinite Intelligence, for the development of the perfect plan which you can, then, persistently follow to achieve your definite purpose, your heart's desire.
—NAPOLEON HILL

What comes from the heart, goes to the heart.
—SAMUEL TAYLOR COLERIDGE

November 9

By utilizing the powers of others'
minds, you add to and multiply the
power of your own.

—NAPOLEON HILL

We are here to add what we can
to, not to get what we can from, life.

—SIR WILLIAM OSLER

November 10

*If you put your mind to work
with a positive mental attitude
and believe in success as your right,
your belief will guide you
unerringly toward whatever your
definition of success may be.*
—NAPOLEON HILL

*Life is action and passion;
therefore, it is required of a man
that he should share the passion
and action of the time, at peril of
being judged not to have lived.*
—OLIVER WENDELL HOLMES

~ Day 314 ~

November 11

If you adopt a negative mental attitude and fill your mind with thoughts of fear and frustration, your mind will attract to you the penalties of these undesirable thoughts.

—NAPOLEON HILL

Our fears are more numerous than our dangers, and we suffer more in our imagination than in reality.

—SENECA

November 12

*Learn to close the door of
your mind on all the failures and
unpleasant circumstances of the
past, and clear your mind so that it
can operate in a positive mental
attitude.*

—NAPOLEON HILL

*If you are distressed by anything
external, the pain is not due to the
thing itself, but to your estimate of
it; and this you have the power to
revoke at any moment.*

–MARCUS AURELIUS

~ Day 316 ~

November 13

Find out what you want most in life and begin getting it, right where you now stand, by helping others to acquire similar benefits, thus putting into action that magic success principle: the habit of going the extra mile.

—NAPOLEON HILL

Joy is not in things. It is in us.

—RICHARD WAGNER

November 14

Select the person who, in your opinion, is the finest person in all the world, past or present, and make that person your pacemaker for the remainder of your life, emulating him or her in every possible way.

—NAPOLEON HILL

Believe one who has tried it.

—VIRGIL

November 15

*Determine how great a supply
of material riches you require, set
up a plan for acquiring it, and then
adopt the principle of not too much,
not too little by which to govern
your future ambition for
material things.*

—NAPOLEON HILL

*I've always been in the right
place at the right time. Of course,
I steered myself there.*

–BOB HOPE

November 16

Form the habit of saying or
doing something every day which
will make another person, or
persons feel better.
—NAPOLEON HILL

Find a need and fill it.
—HENRY J. KAISER

November 17

Make yourself understand that it isn't defeat which whips you, but your mental attitude toward it, and then train yourself to look for the seed of equivalent benefit in each defeat which may come your way.

—NAPOLEON HILL

A man ain't whipped until he quits.

—THOMAS E. GADDIS

November 18

Learn that often when you have
searched in vain for a solution to
your own personal problem, you
can find that solution by helping
someone else solve his
or her problem.

—NAPOLEON HILL

If this stone won't budge at present
and is wedged in, move some of the
other stones round it first.

–LUDWIG WITTGENSTEIN

November 19

The tide seems always to turn in
your favor if you are determined to
see that it does. Your state of
mind has everything to do with
turning the tide.

—NAPOLEON HILL

The right time
comes when one is ready.

—CARL G. JUNG

November 20

Throughout nature we see that every atom of matter and every unit of energy is definitely modified, influenced and sometimes changed entirely by its nearest associates.

—NAPOLEON HILL

All thought is a feat of association: having what's in front of you bring up something in your mind that you almost didn't know you knew.

—ROBERT FROST

November 21

The objects on which you
deliberately concentrate your
attention become the dominating
influences in your environment.
—NAPOLEON HILL

Life consists in what
a man is thinking of all day.
—RALPH WALDO EMERSON

November 22

If your thoughts are fixed upon
poverty, or the physical signs of
poverty, these influences are
transferred to our subconscious
mind through autosuggestion.

—NAPOLEON HILL

I've never been poor, only broke.
Being poor is a frame of mind.
Being broke is only a
temporary situation.

—MIKE TODD

~ Day 326 ~

November 23

If the habit of concentrating on poverty is continued, it will result in conditioning your mind to accept poverty as an unavoidable circumstance, and you will eventually become poverty-conscious.

—NAPOLEON HILL

The real disgrace of poverty is not in owning to the fact but in declining the struggle against it.

—PERICLES

November 24

Controlled attention can be likened
to a gardener who keeps his fertile
garden spot cleared of weeds so that
he can make it yield edible foods.
—NAPOLEON HILL

Let him that would move
the world first move himself.
—SOCRATES

November 25

> One of the most valuable gifts
> you can give any man is the gift
> of direction.
>
> —NAPOLEON HILL

> A word, a look, an accent,
> may affect the destiny not only
> of individuals, but of nations. He
> is a bold man who calls
> anything a trifle.
>
> —ANDREW CARNEGIE

~ Day 329 ~

November 26

Autosuggestion is the tool with which we dig a mental path in the brain. Controlled attention is the hand that holds that tool.
—NAPOLEON HILL

Not everything that is faced can be changed. But nothing can be changed until it is faced.
–JAMES BALDWIN

November 27

Habit is the map or blueprint
which the mental path follows.
—NAPOLEON HILL

Habit simplifies the movements
required to achieve a given result,
makes them more accurate and
diminishes fatigue.
—WILLIAM JAMES

November 28

An idea, or a desire to become
transformed into action, must be
held in the conscious mind until
habit gives it permanent form.
From there on autosuggestion does
the rest by transferring the pattern
to the subconscious mind where it is
taken over and automatically
carried out to its logical conclusion,
by whatever practical means may
be available to the individual.

—NAPOLEON HILL

We carry with us the
wonders we seek without us.

—SIR THOMAS BROWNE

~ Day 332 ~

November 29

Imagination inspires the creation of new combinations both of ideas and material things.
—NAPOLEON HILL

The thoughts that come often unsought, and, as it were, drop into the mind, are commonly the most valuable of any we have.
—JOHN LOCKE

November 30

*One of the common weaknesses
of most of us is that we look with
envy at the men who have attained
noteworthy success, taking stock of
them during the hour of their
triumph without taking note of
the price each had to pay for
his success.*

—NAPOLEON HILL

You can see a lot by just watching.

—YOGI BERRA

~ Day 334 ~

December

If the first plan you adopt
doesn't work successfully,
replace it with a new plan;
if this new plan fails to work,
replace it with still another;
and so on, until you find a
plan that does work.

—NAPOLEON HILL

December 1

Negative thought habits
attract to their creator physical
manifestations corresponding to their
nature as perfectly and as inevitably
as nature germinates the
acorn and develops it
into an oak tree.

—NAPOLEON HILL

We cannot command
nature except by obeying her.

–SIR FRANCIS BACON

December 2

You create patterns of thought by
repeating certain ideas, or behavior,
and the law of cosmic habitforce
takes over those patterns and
makes them more or less permanent
unless or until you consciously
rearrange them.

—NAPOLEON HILL

The best way to stop a
bad habit is never to begin it.

—JAMES C. PENNY

December 3

*Cosmic habitforce does not
directly transmute desires for
money into the coin of the realm,
but it does activate the imagination
to reveal to the individual a way to
make the conversion through
accepted procedure.*

—NAPOLEON HILL

*Too many young people
itch for what they want without
scratching for it.*

–TOM D. TAYLOR

December 4

*Cosmic habitforce imparts a
peculiar quality to your thought
habits which gives you power to
surmount all difficulties, remove all
obstacles, overcome all resistances.*
—NAPOLEON HILL

*Make good habits and
they will make you.*
–PARKS COUSINS

December 5

If your life is not what you want it to be, you will realize that you have drifted into your present condition because you have let the power of cosmic habitforce carry you into the failure side of the river of thought.

—NAPOLEON HILL

The great thing in this world is not so much where we stand, as in what direction we are moving.

—OLIVER WENDELL HOLMES

December 6

*Thoughts which are held in the mind
and repeated act like the cutting head of
a recording machine, making a groove
in the brain, as it were.*

—NAPOLEON HILL

*We've worn into grooves by Time—our
habits. In the end, these grooves are
going to show whether we've been
second rate or champions, each in his
way in dispatching the affairs of every
day. By choosing our habits, we
determine the grooves into which Time
will wear us; and these are grooves that
enrich our lives and make for ease of
mind, peace, happiness—achievement.*

—FRANK B. GILBERTH

December 7

*A job, the opportunity to earn
a livelihood, should be considered
a precious blessing, and toward it
each of us should apply only
positive thinking regarding
the accomplishment and
improvement of our work.*
—NAPOLEON HILL

*The quality of a man's life is in
direct proportion to his commitment
to excellence, regardless of his chosen
field of endeavor.*
—VINCE LOMBARDI

~ Day 341 ~

December 8

Rendering more and better service
in a positive mental attitude toward
your fellow men leads to sound
physical health.

—NAPOLEON HILL

Teach us to give and
not to count the cost.

–IGNATIUS LOYOLA

December 9

When you have a hunch, no
matter how foolish it may seem
put it down on paper.

—NAPOLEON HILL

You get your intuition back
when you make space for it, when
you stop the chattering of the
rational mind.

—ANNE LAMOTT

~ Day 343 ~

December 10

Keep your major purpose and your plans for attaining it to yourself except in connection with your master mind groups.

—NAPOLEON HILL

A secret may be sometimes best kept by keeping the secret of its being a secret.

–HENRY TAYLOR

December 11

A definite major purpose will automatically influence your mind, make it more alert, activate your imagination, increase your enthusiasm and develop your will power.

—NAPOLEON HILL

Higher aims are in themselves more valuable, even if unfulfilled, than lower ones quite attained.

—JOHANN VON GOETHE

~ Day 345 ~

December 12

*A burning desire is a desire
which is so strong that you believe
yourself already in possession of its
objective even before you actually
start to acquire it.*
—NAPOLEON HILL

*Where there is great love,
there are always miracles.*
–WILLA CATHER

December 13

For it is clear that any fixed purpose becomes a definite part of one's thought habits and, as such, is carried out to its logical climax through the fixation of those habits.
—NAPOLEON HILL

To fall into a habit is to begin to cease to be.
—MIGUEL DE UNAMUNO Y JUGO

December 14

The principle by which an idea germinates and grows and becomes a habit has been designated as cosmic habitforce.

—Napoleon Hill

This is the true joy in life, the being used for a purpose recognized by yourself as a mighty one; the being thoroughly worn out before you are thrown on the scrapheap; the being a force of Nature instead of a feverish, selfish, little clod of ailments and grievances complaining that the world will not devote itself to making you happy.

—George Bernard Shaw

December 15

Men are all born equal in the
sense that they have equal access
to this great principle.

—Napoleon Hill

We are all children of one
and the same God and, therefore,
absolutely equal.

–Mohandas K. Gandhi

~ Day 349 ~

December 16

Control your mental attitude, keep it
positive by exercising self-discipline,
and thus prepare the mental soil in
which any worthwhile plan, purpose
or desire may be planted by repeated,
intense impression, with the
assurance that it will germinate,
grow and find expression ultimately
in its material equivalent, through
whatever means at hand.

—NAPOLEON HILL

I am part of all that I have met.

—ALFRED LORD TENNYSON

~ Day 350 ~

December 17

The accurate thinker is not the slave, but the master, of his own emotions.

—NAPOLEON HILL

No one can be a great thinker who does not recognize that as a thinker it is his first duty to follow his intellect to whatever conclusions it may lead.

–JOHN STUART MILL

December 18

Therefore, in its simplest form,
self-discipline causes you to think
first and act afterward.

—NAPOLEON HILL

Self-command is not only itself
a great virtue, but from it all the
other virtues seem to derive their
principle luster.

—ADAM SMITH

December 19

Learn to relate yourself to every circumstance which influences your life as something which happened for the best, for it may well be that your saddest experience will bring you your greatest assets if you will give time a chance to mellow the experience.

—NAPOLEON HILL

We were deliberately designed to learn by trial and error.

—BUCKMINSTER FULLER

December 20

The only way a man can explain
away his failure is by trimming his
sails, through self-discipline, so that
the later circumstances of his life
will lead him to success.

—NAPOLEON HILL

Don't find fault—find a remedy.

–HENRY FORD

December 21

Going the extra mile turns the spotlight on you and gives you the benefit of the law of contrast, which is very important in advertising yourself.

—NAPOLEON HILL

Every one to whom much is given, of him will much be required.

–JESUS

December 22

You cannot succeed in life by scattering your forces and trying to do a dozen things at the same time.
—NAPOLEON HILL

Everybody thinks of changing humanity and nobody thinks of changing himself.
—LEO TOLSTOY

December 23

The creative force of the entire universe functions through your mind when you establish a definite purpose and apply your faith to its fulfillment.

—NAPOLEON HILL

The creation of a thousand forests is in one acorn.

–RALPH WALDO EMERSON

~ Day 357 ~

December 24

*The one way to separate yourself
from the mass of humanity and
climb out of mediocrity to stardom
is—not to journey to some desert or
forgotten island, or lock yourself in
solitary confinement—but to hitch
your wagon to the star of some
strong purpose.*

—NAPOLEON HILL

*First say to yourself what
you would be, and then do what
you have to do.*

—EPICTETUS

December 25

Keep your mind on the things you want and off the things you don't want.

—NAPOLEON HILL

A man must make his opportunity, as oft as find it.

—SIR FRANCIS BACON

December 26

*If you make your prayers an
expression of gratitude and
thanksgiving for the blessings you
have already received, instead of
requests for what you do not have,
you will obtain results a great
deal faster.*

—NAPOLEON HILL

Gratitude is the sign of noble souls.

—AESOP

~ Day 360 ~

December 27

You may be confident that if your purpose is right and worthy, is not calculated to harm or destroy, is not contrary to the laws of nature: your faith cannot fail.

—NAPOLEON HILL

If we can change our thoughts, we can change the world.

–H. M. TOMLINSON

December 28

You must give an equivalent
value for the object of your desire.
—NAPOLEON HILL

Everything is worth what
its purchaser will pay for it.
—PUBLILIUS SYRUS

December 29

The law of reaping increased
returns by rendering more and
better service than that for which
you are paid is one of the basic laws
of nature and had been recognized
by scientists and philosophers
for centuries.

—Napoleon Hill

The habit of giving only
enhances the desire to give.

—Walt Whitman

December 30

Every seed brings forth after its kind. Be sure to include in the seed of your desire some love of your fellowman, some of the milk of human kindness.
—NAPOLEON HILL

Live truth instead of expressing it.
—ELBERT HUBBARD

December 31

*Faith is the greatest
power known to man.*
—NAPOLEON HILL

*Nothing in life is to be feared.
It is only to be understood.*
—MARIE CURIE

For additional information about Napoleon Hill products please contact the following locations:

Napoleon Hill World Learning Center
Purdue University Calumet
2300 173rd Street
Hammond, IN 46323-2094

Judith Williamson, Director
Uriel "Chino" Martinez, Assistant/Graphic Designer

Telephone: 219-989-3173 or 219-989-3166
email: nhf@calumet.purdue.edu

Napoleon Hill Foundation
University of Virginia-Wise
College Relations Apt. C
1 College Avenue
Wise, VA 24293

Don Green, Executive Director
Annedia Sturgill, Executive Assistant

Telephone: 276-328-6700
email: napoleonhill@uvawise.edu

Website: www.naphill.org

Made in the USA
Monee, IL
26 March 2024

55827528R00225